CURRENT HITS ON
Broadway

ISBN 978-1-4803-9387-5

HAL•LEONARD® CORPORATION
7777 W. BLUEMOUND RD. P.O. BOX 13819 MILWAUKEE, WI 53213

Visit Hal Leonard Online at
www.halleonard.com

A WHOLE NEW WORLD
from Disney ALADDIN

Music by ALAN MENKEN
Lyrics by TIM RICE

(You Make Me Feel Like)
A NATURAL WOMAN
from BEAUTIFUL

Words and Music by GERRY GOFFIN,
CAROLE KING and JERRY WEXLER

WILL YOU LOVE ME TOMORROW
(Will You Still Love Me Tomorrow)
from BEAUTIFUL

Words and Music by GERRY GOFFIN
and CAROLE KING

I BELIEVE

from the Broadway Musical THE BOOK OF MORMON

Words and Music by TREY PARKER,
ROBERT LOPEZ and MATT STONE
Vocal Arrangement by STEPHEN OREMUS

Majestically

Colla voce

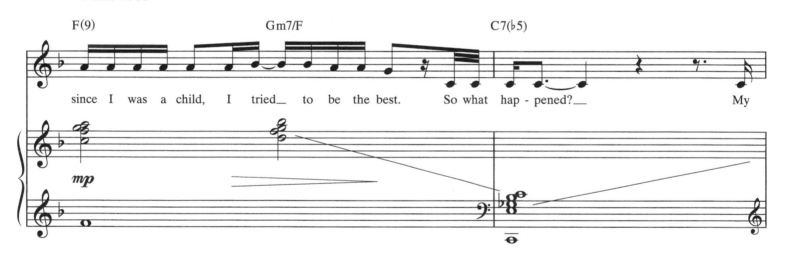

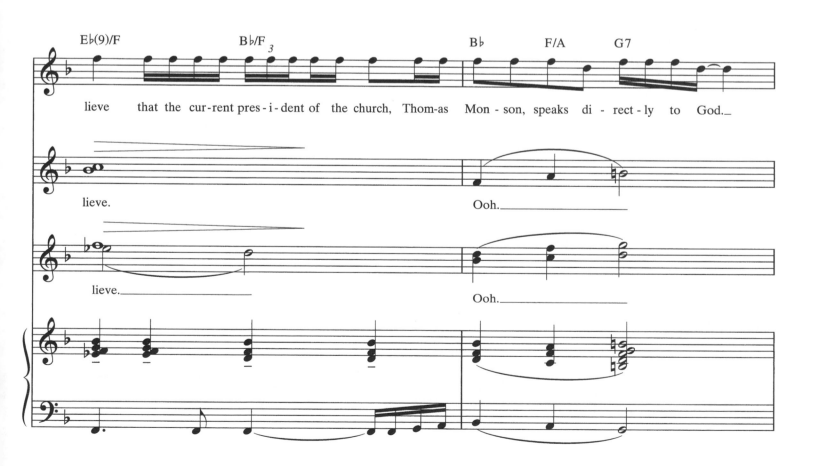

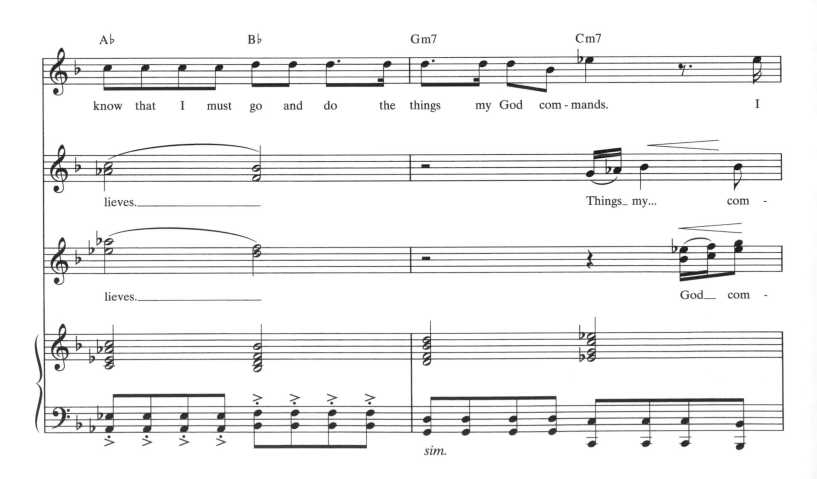

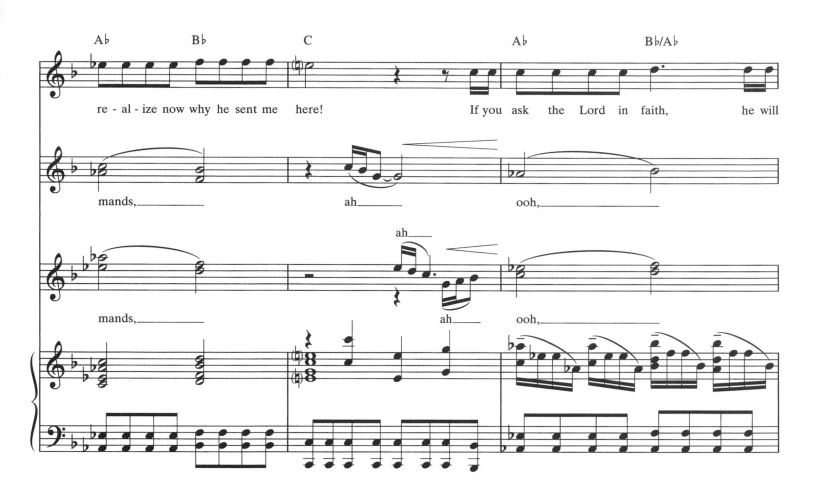

lieve that in Nine-teen-Sev-en-ty-eight, God changed his mind_ a-bout black peo-ple._

lieve, ooh,_____ black peo-ple!_

lieve,_____ ooh,_____ black peo-ple!_

You can be a Mor-mon, a Mor-mon who just be -

You can be a Mor-mon, a Mor-mon who just be -

You can be a Mor-mon, a Mor-mon who just be -

General: *The fuck is this?*

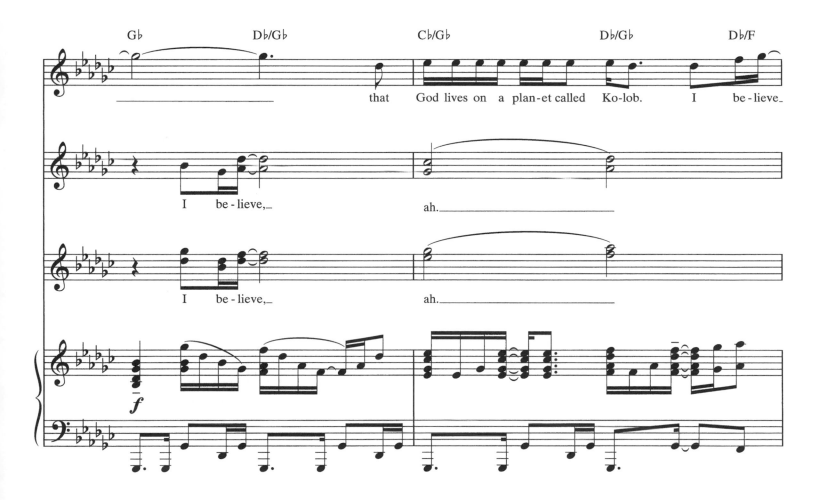

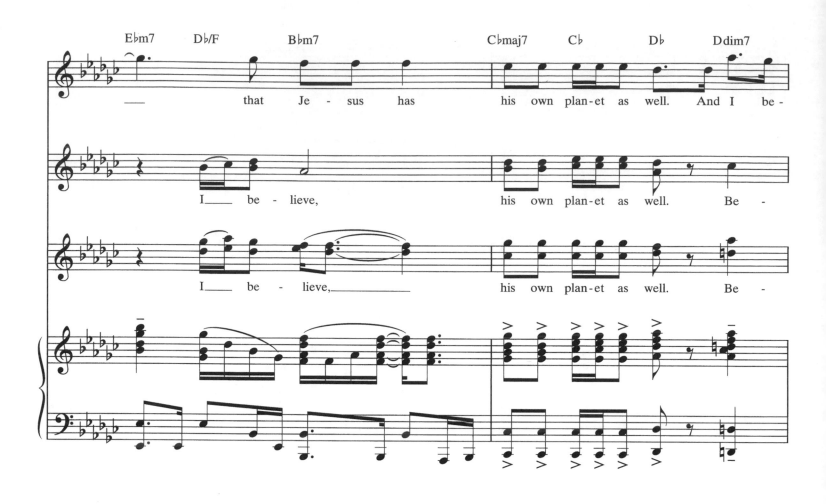

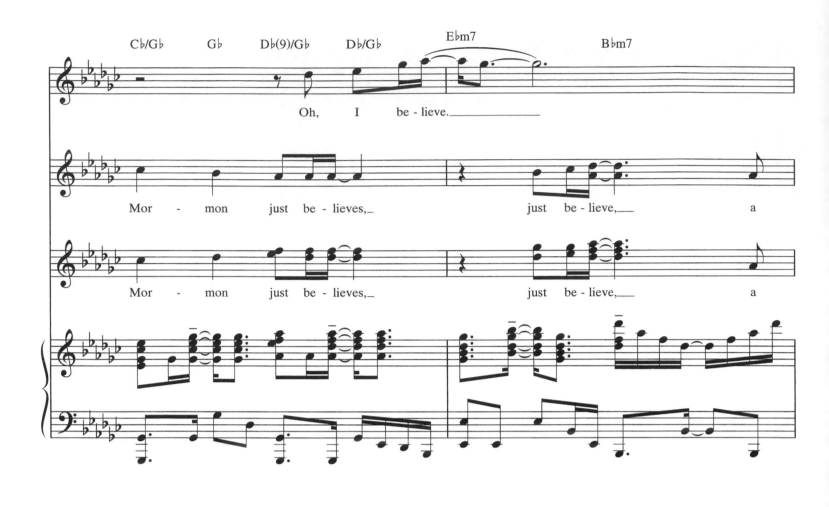

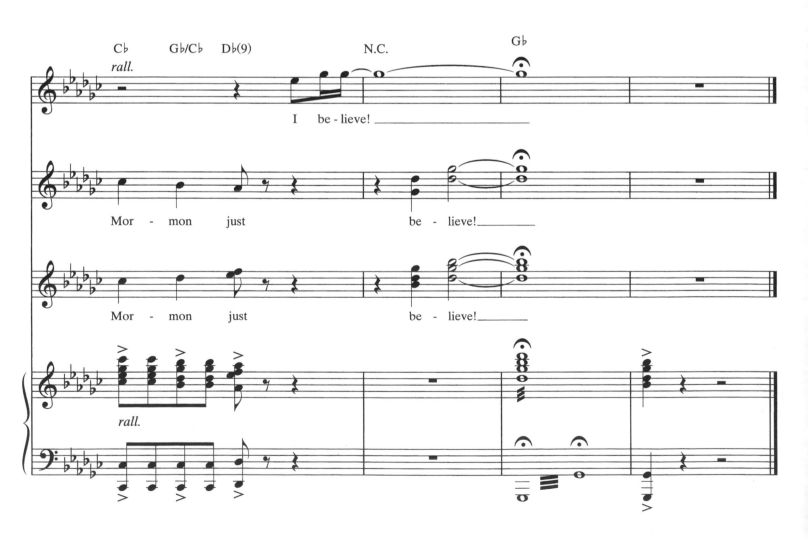

YOU AND ME
(But Mostly Me)
from the Broadway Musical THE BOOK OF MORMON

Words and Music by TREY PARKER, MATT STONE
and ROBERT LOPEZ
Vocal Arrangement by STEPHEN OREMUS

Now it's our___ time to___ go out and set the world's peo - ple free.

Elder Cunningham:

My best friend.

And we can do___ it to - geth - er, you___ and me,

Bright rock (♩ = 152)

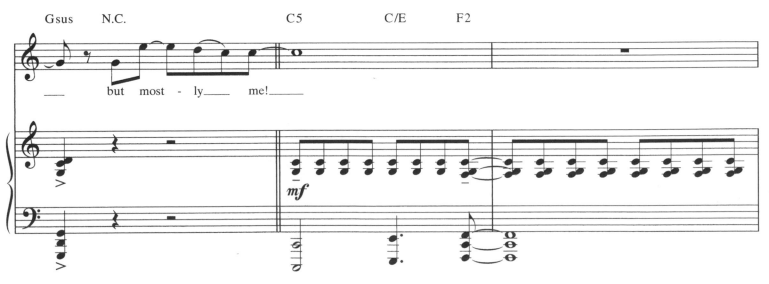

___ but most - ly___ me!___

Dreamy, with half-time feel

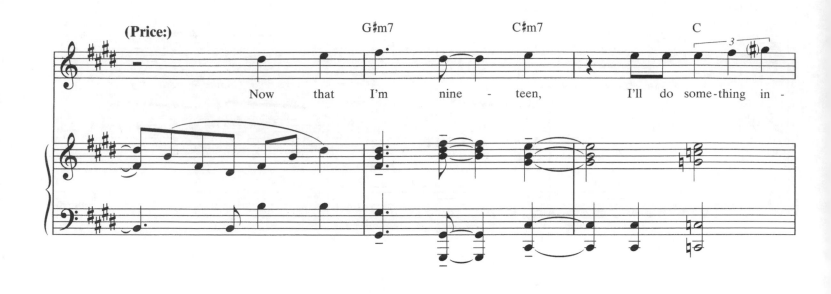

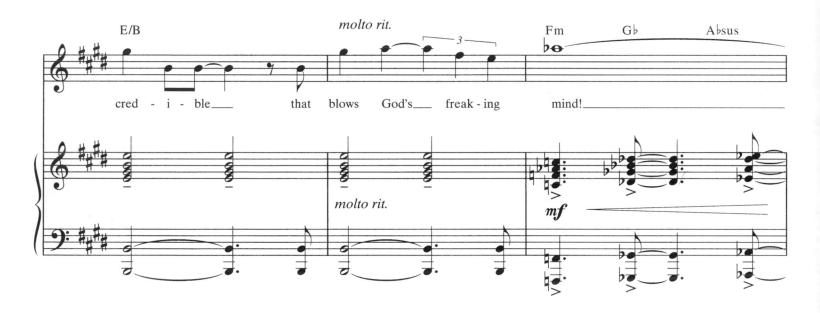

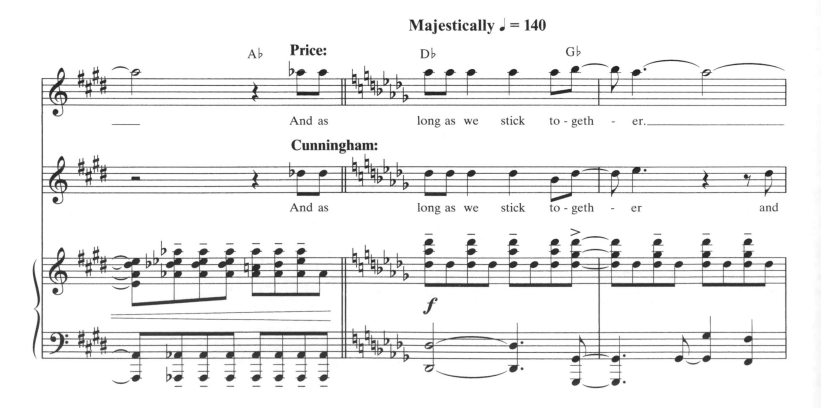

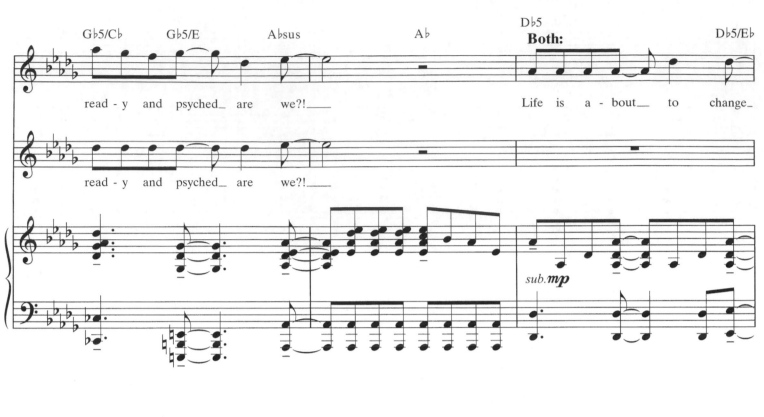

read-y and psyched_ are we?!___ Life is a-bout_ to change_

read-y and psyched_ are we?!___

Price /
Cunningham:

___ for you.___ And life is a-bout_ to change_ for me. And

life is a-bout_ to change_ for you_ and me,___ but me___ most-

LET'S MISBEHAVE

from BULLETS OVER BROADWAY

Words and Music by
COLE PORTER

You could have __ a great ca - reer, __ and you should. __

AND ALL THAT JAZZ
from CHICAGO

Words by FRED EBB
Music by JOHN KANDER

Moderately

Come on, babe, _ why don't we paint the town, _ and all that jazz! _ I'm gon-na

rouge my knees _ and roll my stock-ings down _ and all that jazz! _

Start the car, _ I know a whoop-ee spot _ where the gin is cold _ but the pi - an - o's hot. _ It's just a

I'VE DECIDED TO MARRY YOU

from A GENTLEMAN'S GUIDE TO LOVE & MURDER

Music by STEVEN LUTVAK
Lyrics by ROBERT L. FREEDMAN and
STEVEN LUTVAK

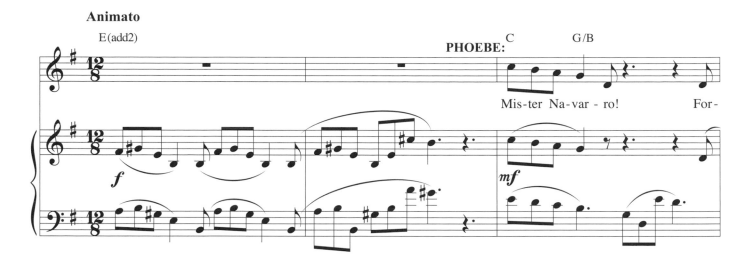

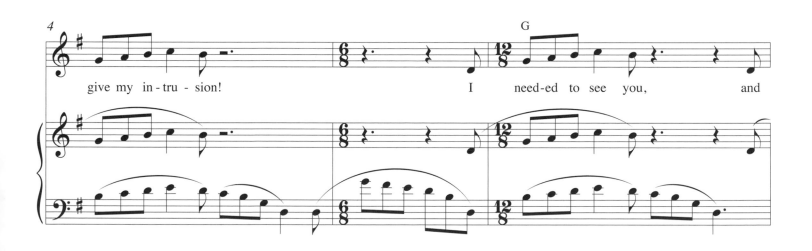

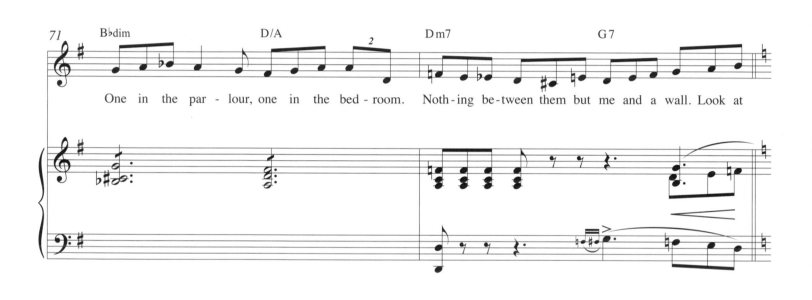

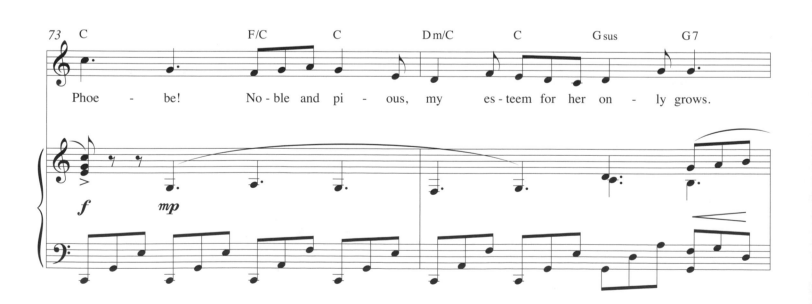

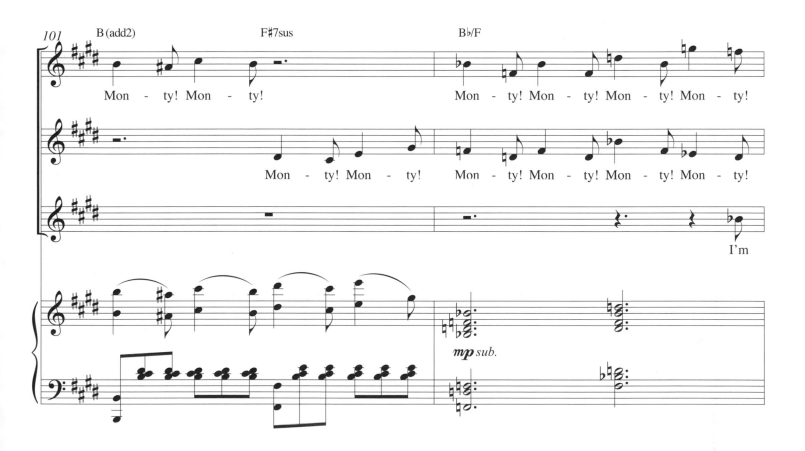

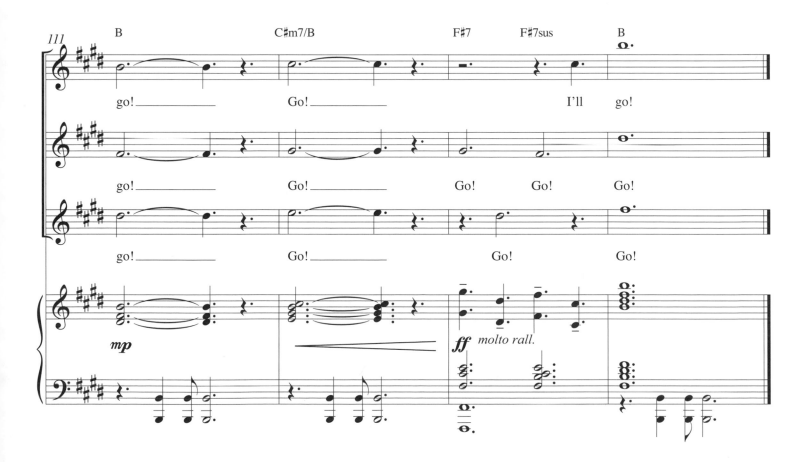

POISON IN MY POCKET

from A GENTLEMAN'S GUIDE TO LOVE & MURDER

Music by STEVEN LUTVAK
Lyrics by ROBERT L. FREEDMAN and
STEVEN LUTVAK

(Asquith Jr. and Miss Barley
fall through the ice and drown.)

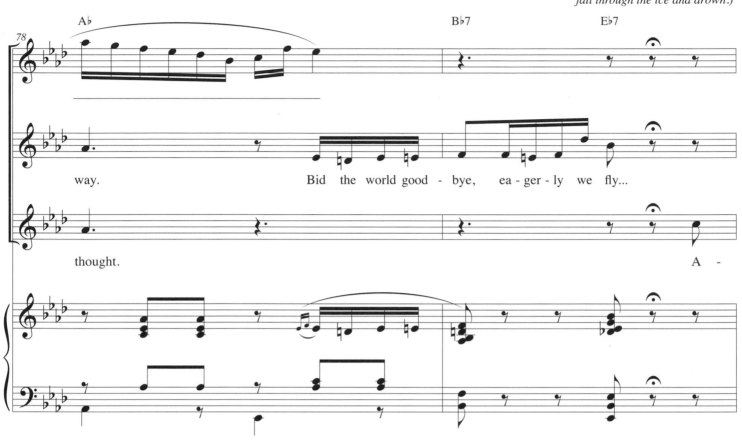

way.   Bid the world good - bye,   ea - ger - ly we fly...

thought.   A -

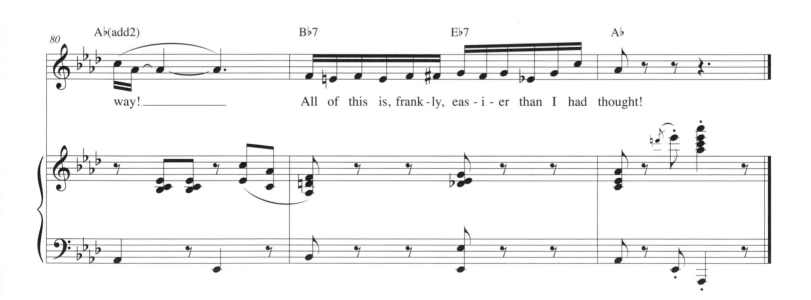

way!_____   All of this is, frank - ly, eas - i - er than I had thought!

THE ORIGIN OF LOVE
from HEDWIG AND THE ANGRY INCH

Words and Music by
STEPHEN TRASK

D.S. al Coda

the or - i - gin of love.

Now the

CODA

right up in half." And the storm clouds gath - ered a - bove

cresc.

in - to great balls of fi - re.

And then fi -

re shot down from the sky in bolts,

Additional Lyrics

2. Now the gods grew quite scared
   Of our strength and defiance,
   And Thor said, "I'm gonna kill 'em all with my hammer,
   Like I killed the giants."
   But Zeus said, "No, you better let me use my lightning like scissors,
   Like I cut the legs off the whales, dinosaurs into lizards."
   And then he grabbed up some bolts
   And he let out a laugh,
   Said, "I'll split them right down the middle.
   Gonna cut 'em right up in half."

WIG IN A BOX
from HEDWIG AND THE ANGRY INCH

Words and Music by
STEPHEN TRASK

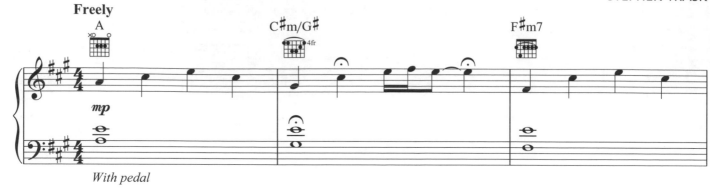

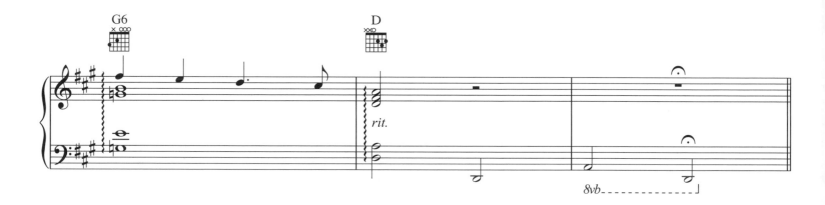

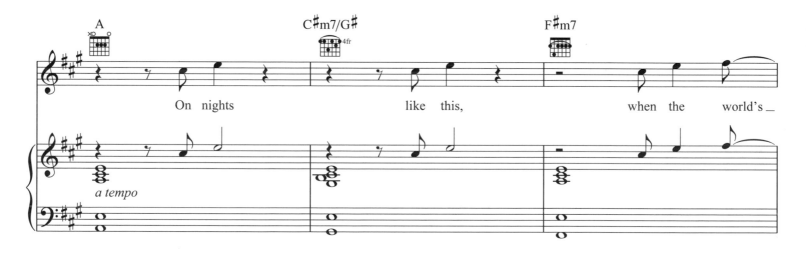

On nights   like this,   when the world's _

_ a   bit a - miss   and the lights go down _ a-

the gift-wrapped wig still in the box _____ of
this is the best way that I've found _____ to be the

tow - er - ing vel - ve - teen. _____ I put on some make - up,
best _____ you've ev - er seen. _____ I put on some make - up,
I put on some make - up,

some La - Vern Bak - er, and pull the wig _____
turn on the eight - track. I'm pull - ing the wig _____
turn on the eight - track. I'm pull - ing the wig _____

*Female vocal written one octave higher than sung.

NOT MY FATHER'S SON

from the Broadway Musical KINKY BOOTS

Words and Music by
CYNTHIA LAUPER

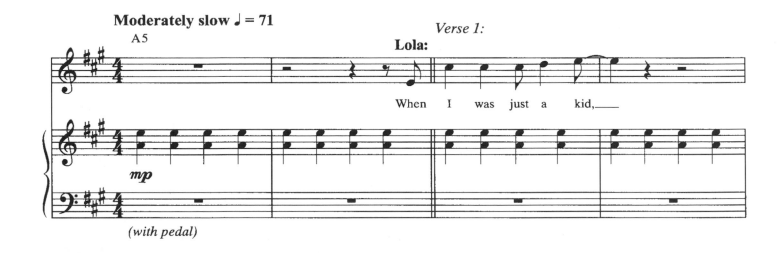

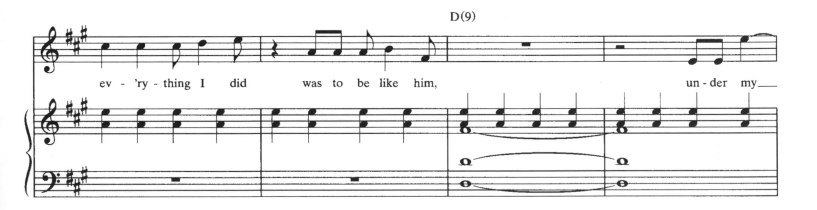

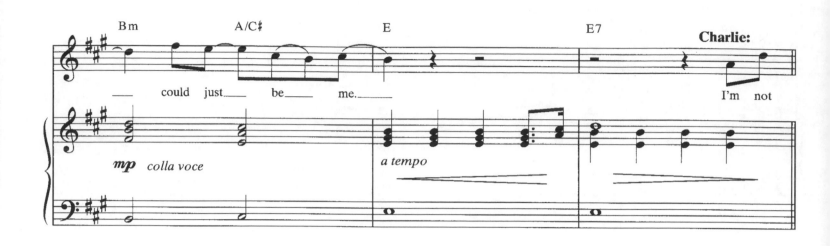

could just___ be___ me.___

Charlie:
I'm not

Chorus:

my fath - er's son___ I'm not the im - age of

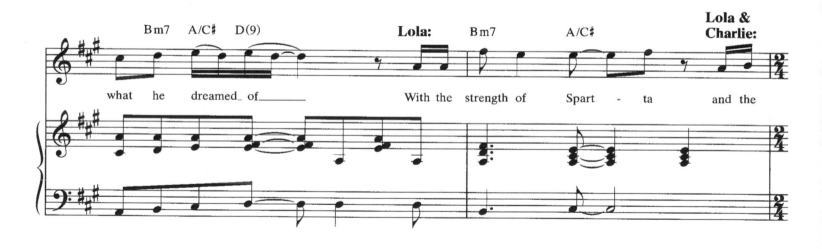

what he dreamed_ of_____

Lola:
With the strength of Spar - ta and the

Lola & Charlie:

pat - ience of Job,_____ still could - n't be the one___

to ech - o what he'd done_____ and mir - ror

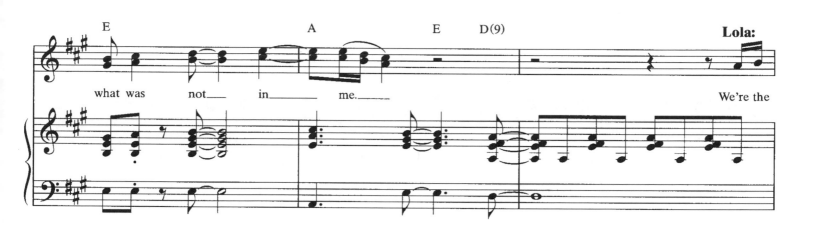

what was not___ in___ me.___

Lola:

We're the

Slightly slower

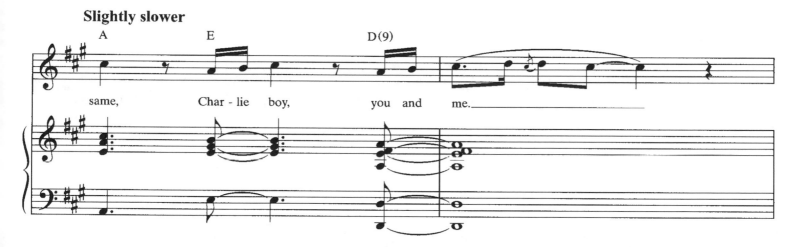

same, Char - lie boy, you and me._____

Lola: *Charlie from Northampton, meet Simon from Clacton.*
Charlie: *Let's make boots!*

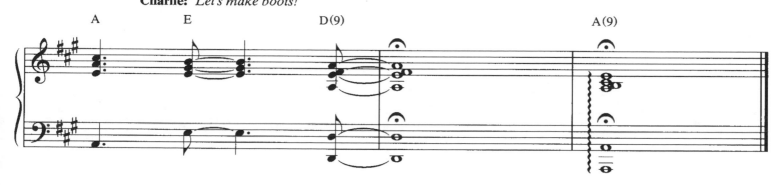

RAISE YOU UP/JUST BE

from the Broadway Musical KINKY BOOTS

Words and Music by
CYNTHIA LAUPER

Lauren: *Wait! Wait! Wait! Wait! Hold it right there buster. Are you saying you'd like to take me out?*
Charlie: *Yes.*
Lauren: *Are you saying that you and Nicola are through?*
Charlie: *Yes.*
Lauren: *Are you saying that you are actually available?*
Charlie: *Yes.*
Lauren: *And you still like girls?*
Charlie: *Yes.*
Lauren: *Carry on!*

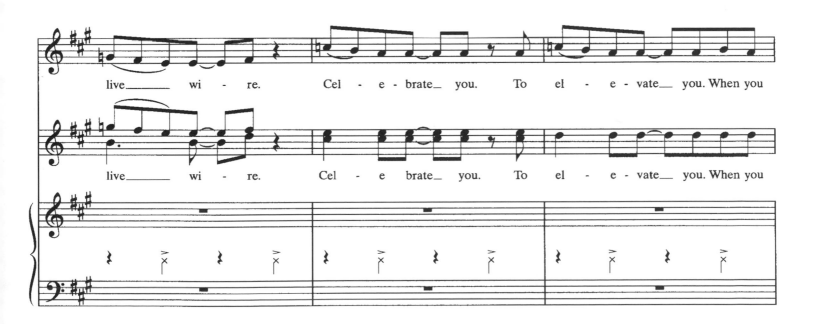

strug - gle to stand, well, take a help - ing hand. If you

strug - gle to stand, well, take a help - ing hand. If you

All Women:

hit the dust,___ let me raise you up.___ When your bub - ble busts,___ let me

Angels:

hit the dust,___ let me raise you up.___ When your bub - ble busts,___ let me

Tenors2/ Baritones:

hit the dust,___ let me raise you up.___ When your bub - ble busts,___ let me

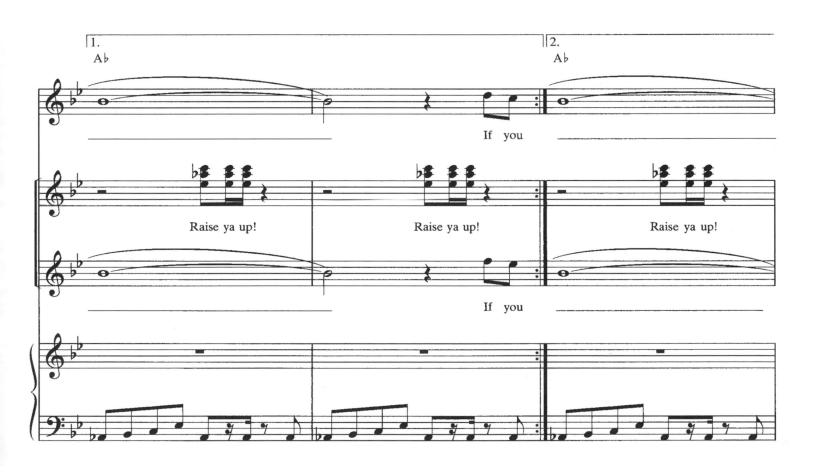

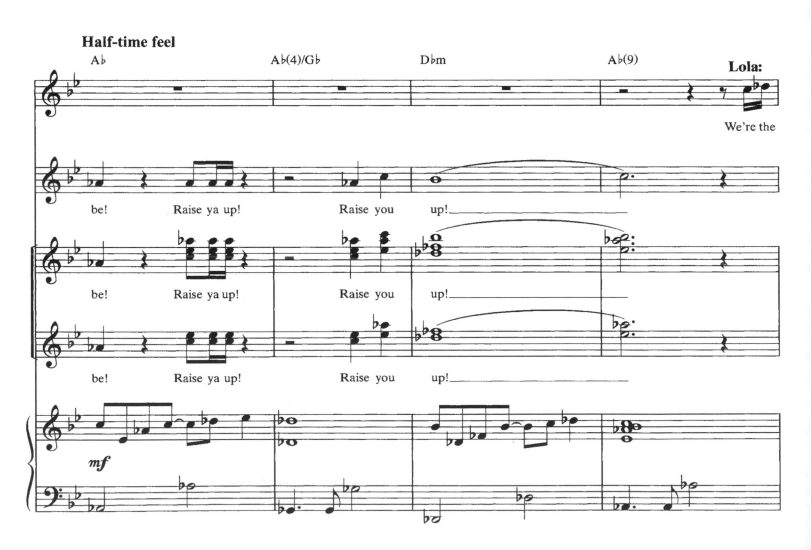

131

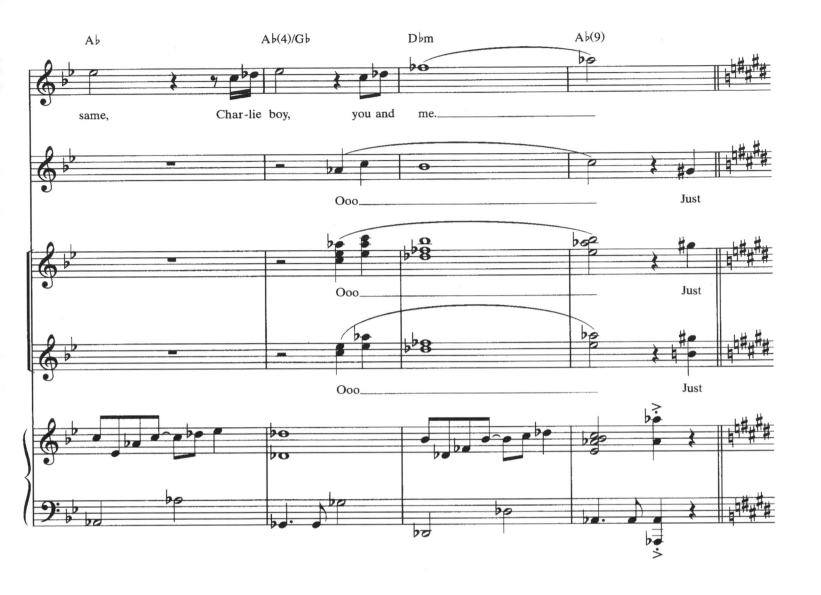

Groove!

Lola: *Ladies...*
Charlie: *Gentlemen...*
Both: *...and those who have yet to make up their minds.*

Charlie: *As people all over the world clamor for Kinky Boots... it is time for us to get back to work. But before we go, we'd like to leave you with the 'Price & Simon secret to success.*
Lola: *Alright, now we've all heard of the Twelve Step program have we not, yes? Well, what you can do in twelve, I want you to know that we all can do in six.*

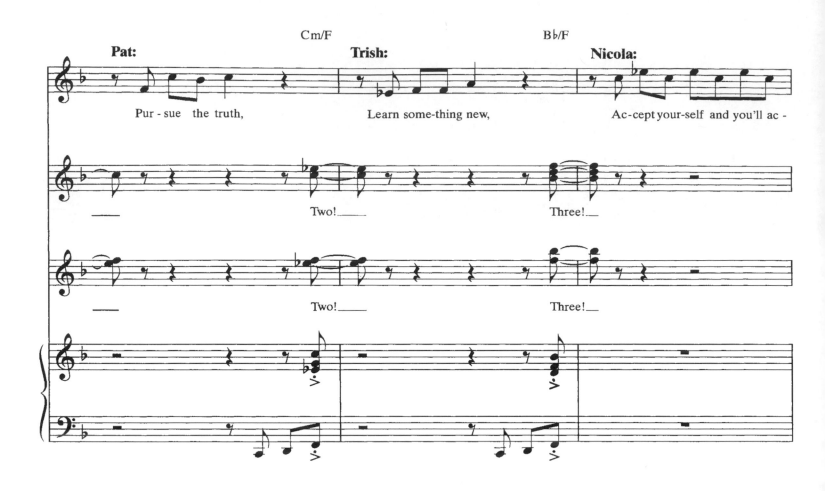

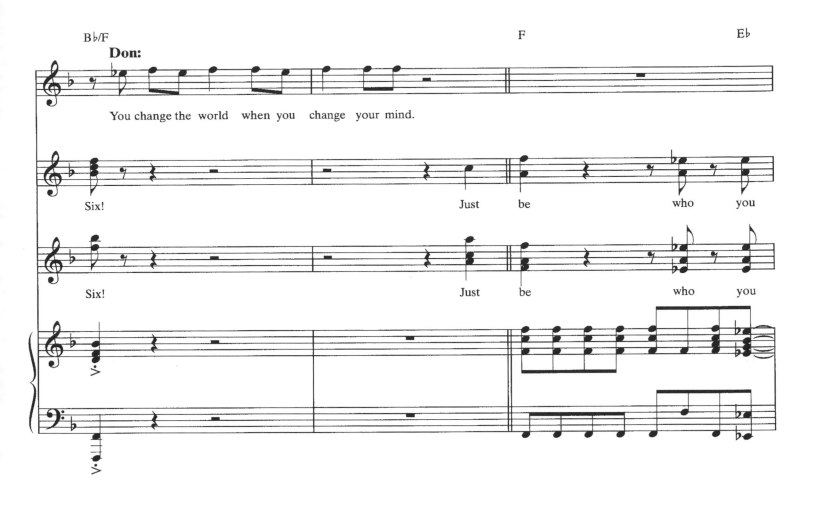

You change the world when you change your mind.

Six!

Just be who you

Six!

Just be who you

(Women:)

wan - na be. Nev - er let 'em tell you who you ought. to be. Just

(Men:)

wan - na be. Nev - er let 'em tell you who you ought. to be. Just

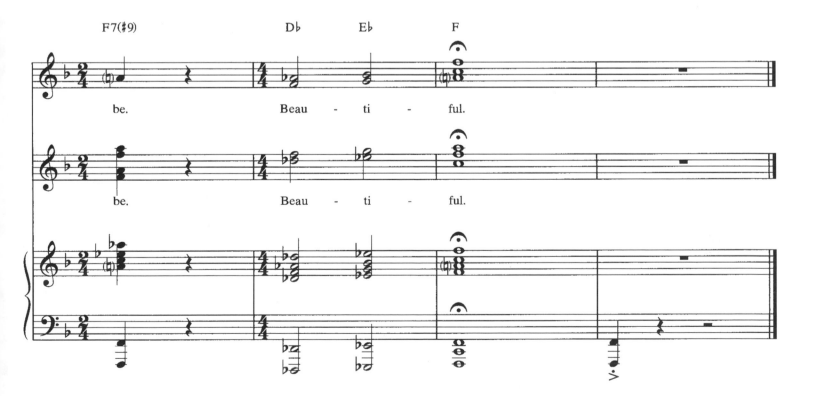

ON MY OWN

from LES MISÉRABLES

Music by CLAUDE-MICHEL SCHÖNBERG
Lyrics by ALAIN BOUBLIL, JEAN-MARC NATEL,
HERBERT KRETZMER, JOHN CAIRD
and TREVOR NUNN

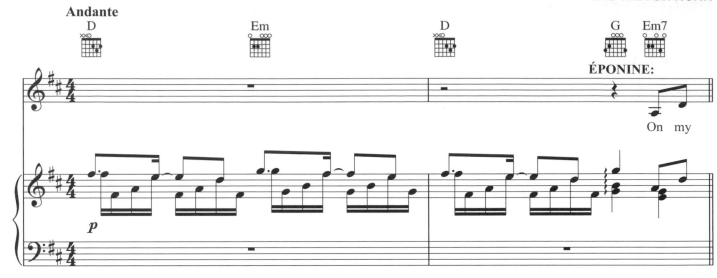

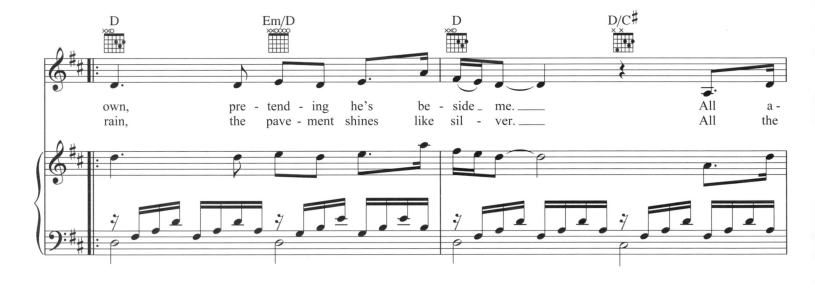

DANCING QUEEN

from MAMMA MIA!

Words and Music by BENNY ANDERSSON,
BJÖRN ULVAEUS and STIG ANDERSON

Watch that __ scene, __ dig - gin' the danc - ing __ queen. __

Dig-gin' the

danc - ing __ queen. _____

Repeat and Fade

THE WINNER TAKES IT ALL

from MAMMA MIA!

Words and Music by BENNY ANDERSSON
and BJÖRN ULVAEUS

I don't wan - na talk
arms kiss
talk

a - bout things we've gone through,
think - ing I be - longed there,
like I used to kiss you,
if it makes you feel sad,

though it's hurt - ing
I fig - ured it made
does it feel the
and I un - der-

To Coda

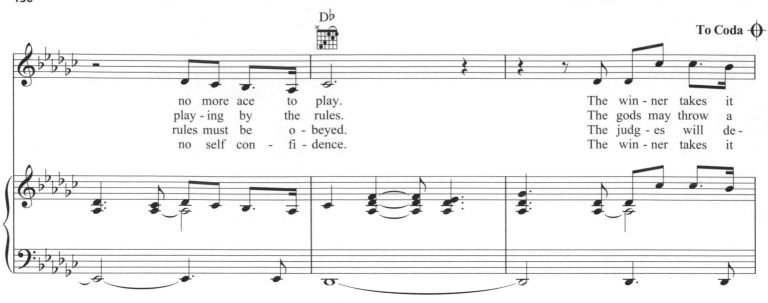

no more ace   to   play.
play - ing by   the   rules.
rules must be   o - beyed.
no self con - fi - dence.

The win - ner takes   it
The gods may throw a
The judg - es will de -
The win - ner takes   it

all,   the los - er stand - ing   small
dice,   their minds as cold as   ice,
cide,   the likes of me a - bide,

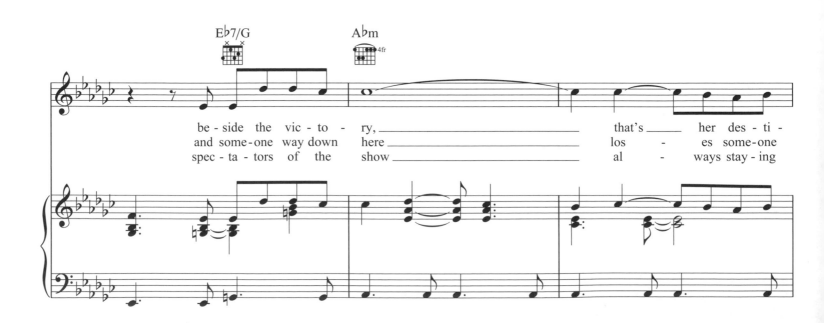

be - side the vic - to - ry, _____ that's ____ her des - ti -
and some - one way down here _____ los - es some - one
spec - ta - tors of the show _____ al - ways stay - ing

Naughty
from MATILDA THE MUSICAL

Words and Music by
TIM MINCHIN

what if you have-n't got a fair-y to fix it? Some-times you have to make a lit-tle bit of mis-

- chief!

Just be-cause you find that life's__ not fair,__ it does-n't mean that you just have to grin and bear__ it.

If you al-ways take it on the chin and wear it, noth-ing will change.

WHEN I GROW UP
from MATILDA THE MUSICAL

Words and Music by
TIM MINCHIN

164

AIN'T NO MOUNTAIN HIGH ENOUGH
from MOTOWN THE MUSICAL

Words and Music by NICKOLAS ASHFORD
and VALERIE SIMPSON

I HEARD IT THROUGH THE GRAPEVINE

from MOTOWN THE MUSICAL

Words and Music by NORMAN J. WHITFIELD
and BARRETT STRONG

Mmm, _____ I bet you're won-d'ring how I knew ba-by, ba - by, ba-

by, 'bout your plans to __ make me blue _____ with some oth-er girl you

knew be-fore. Be - tween the two __ of us girls, you know I love you more. __

SANTA FE
from Disney's NEWSIES THE MUSICAL

Music by ALAN MENKEN
Lyrics by JACK FELDMAN

With more drive

Where does it say you got - ta live and die here? _____

Where does it say a guy can't catch a break?

Why should you on - ly take what you're giv - en? Why should you spend your whole life liv - in'

poco accel.

Solidly, slightly faster

trapped where there ain't no fu - ture, e - ven at sev - en - teen,

paint - in' in my head. 'Cause I'm dead if I can't

count on you to - day. _____ I got

noth - in', if I don't got San - ta Fe. _____

Briskly

SEIZE THE DAY
from Disney's NEWSIES THE MUSICAL

Music by ALAN MENKEN
Lyrics by JACK FELDMAN

Gentle Hymn

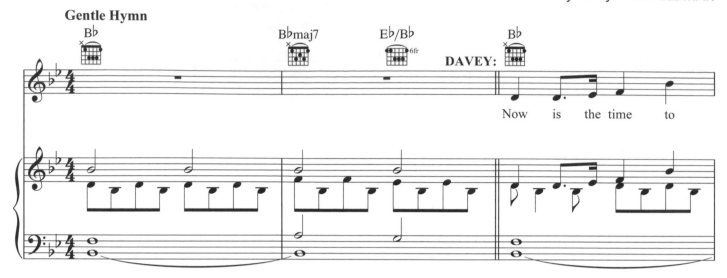

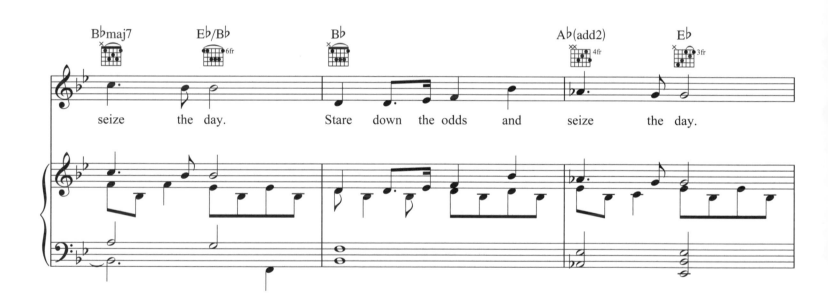

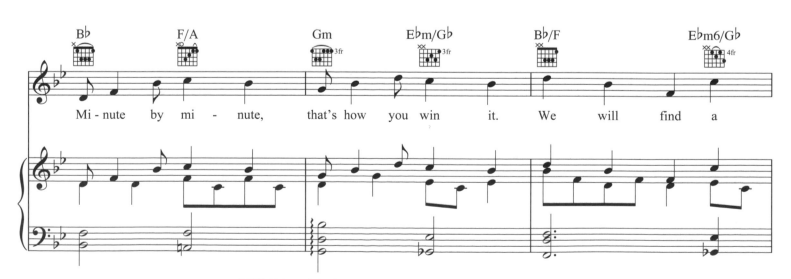

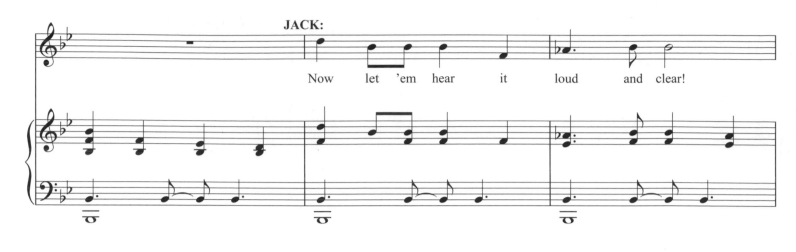

JACK:

Now let 'em hear it loud and clear!

NEWSIES & DAVEY:

Now let 'em hear it loud and clear!

JACK:

Like it or not, we're

NEWSIES & DAVEY:

draw - ing near! Like it or not, we're draw - ing near!

Proud and __ de - fi - ant, we'll slay __ the gi - ant!

FALLING SLOWLY

from the Broadway Musical ONCE

Words and Music by GLEN HANSARD
and MARKETA IRGLOVA

Am   G6   Fsus2   Fsus2

self;   it's   time that you   won. _

cresc.

C   Fsus2   Am7

Take   this   sink - in'   boat   and   point   it   home,   we've   still   got

mf

Fsus2   C   Fsus2

time. _____   Raise   your   hope - ful   voice;   you   have   a

Am7   Fsus2   C

choice,   you've   make   it   now. _____   Fall - in'   slow - ly,

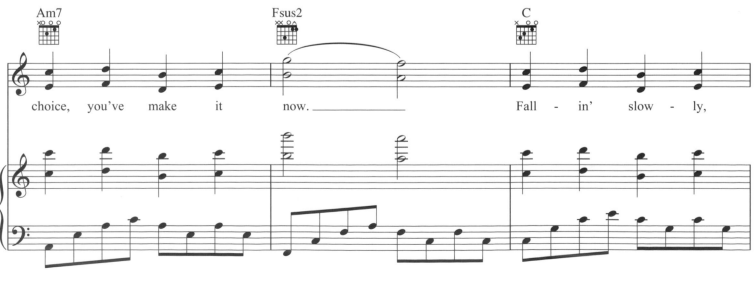

sing your mel - o - dy; I'll sing it loud.

(Strings)

Take it all.

I paid the cost too late,

Now you're gone. ___

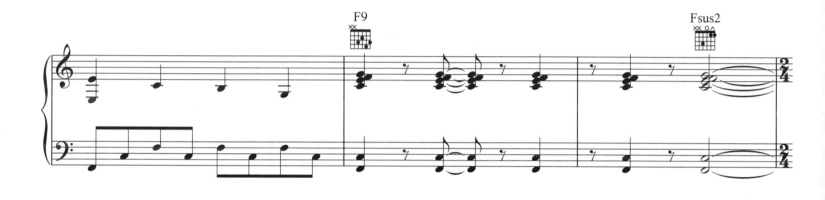

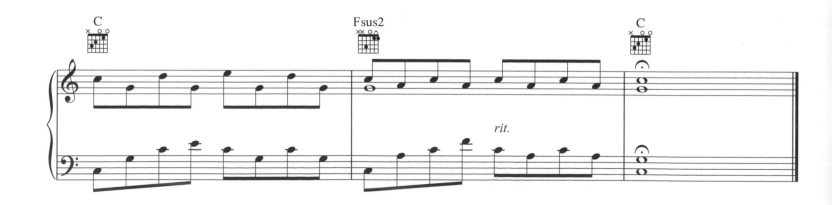

CORNER OF THE SKY

from PIPPIN

Music and Lyrics by
STEPHEN SCHWARTZ

MORNING GLOW

from PIPPIN

Music and Lyrics by
STEPHEN SCHWARTZ

Nice steady rock tempo

Suddenly faster

Morn-ing glow is here_____

at

last._____

DON'T STOP BELIEVIN'

from ROCK OF AGES

Words and Music by STEVE PERRY,
NEAL SCHON and JONATHAN CAIN

She took the mid-night train ___ go - in'
He took the mid-night train ___ go - in'

an - y - where. ___

an - y - where. ___

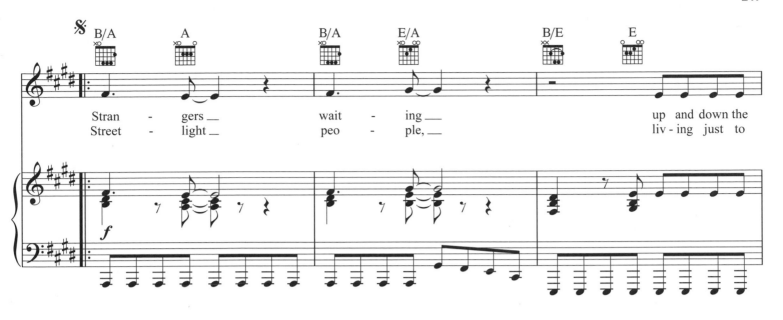

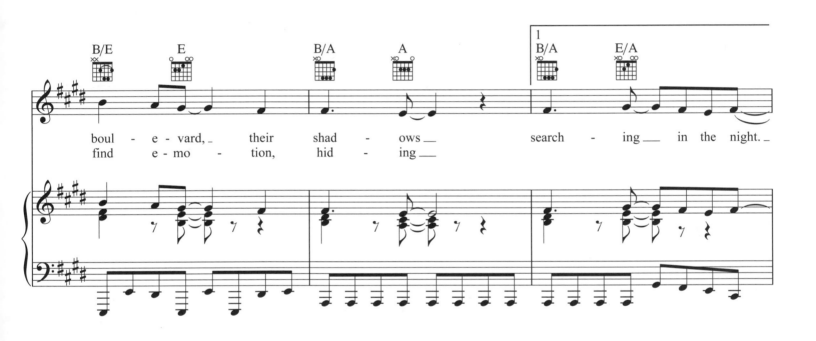

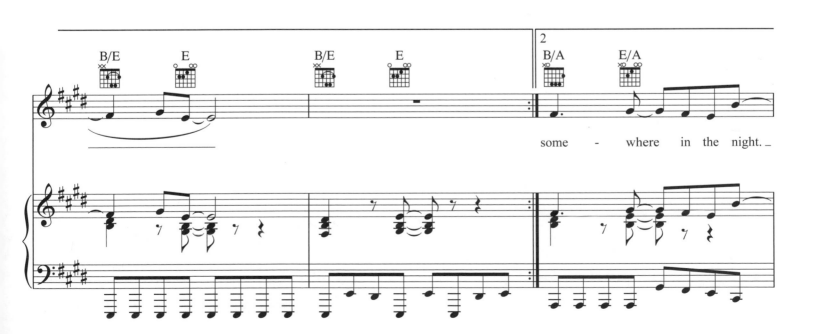

Work-in' hard __ to get my fill. __ Ev-'ry-bod - y

wants a thrill. ____ Pay - in' an - y - thing to roll the dice __ just

Repeat and Fade

POUR SOME SUGAR ON ME

from ROCK OF AGES

Words and Music by JOE ELLIOTT, PHIL COLLEN,
RICHARD SAVAGE, RICHARD ALLEN,
STEVE CLARK and R.J. LANGE

Love is like a bomb, ba - by; come on, get it on.
Red - a light, yel - low light, green - a light, go,

Liv - in' like a lov - er with a ra - dar phone. Look - in' like a tramp, like a vid - e - o vamp.
cra - zy lit - tle wom - an in a one - man show. Mir - ror queen, man - ne - quin, rhy - thm of love,

Dem - o - li - tion wom - an, can I be your man?
sweet dream, sac - cha - rine, loos - en up.

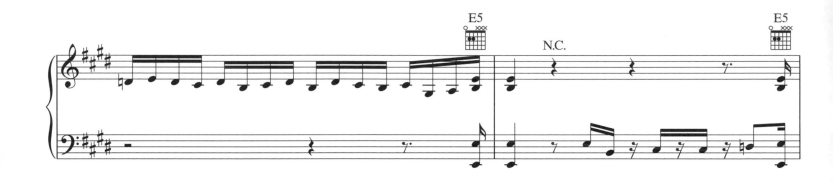

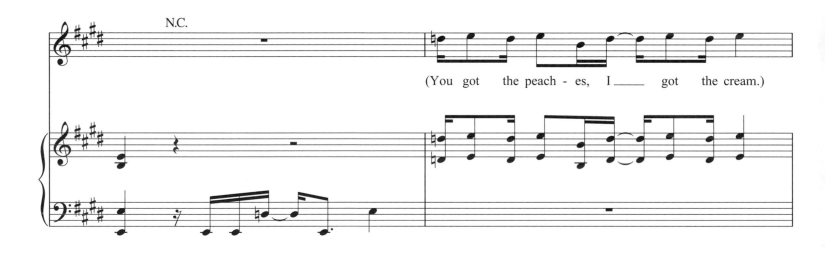

(You got   the peach - es,   I ____   got   the cream.)

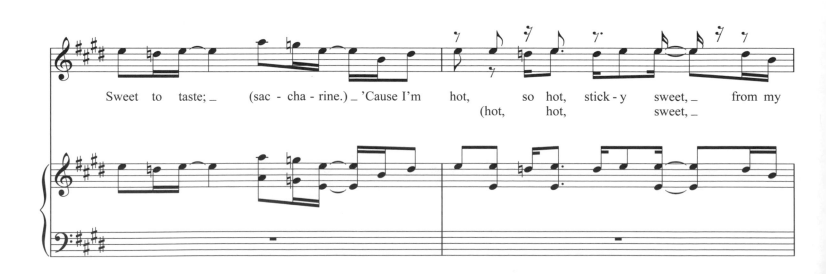

Sweet   to   taste; __   (sac - cha - rine.) __ 'Cause I'm   hot,   so hot,   stick-y   sweet, __   from my
(hot,   hot,   sweet, __

FIGHT FROM THE HEART
from ROCKY BROADWAY

Lyrics by LYNN AHRENS
Music by STEPHEN FLAHERTY

But I'm hear-ing your voice in my head say-in', "Don't let this go.

What you got in you, there's still time to know."

I hear you say-in' _____ tear it a - part! _____

Fight with-out __ think-in' and fight with-out __ shame.

DEFYING GRAVITY
from the Broadway Musical WICKED

Music and Lyrics by
STEPHEN SCHWARTZ

Freely, with quiet intensity

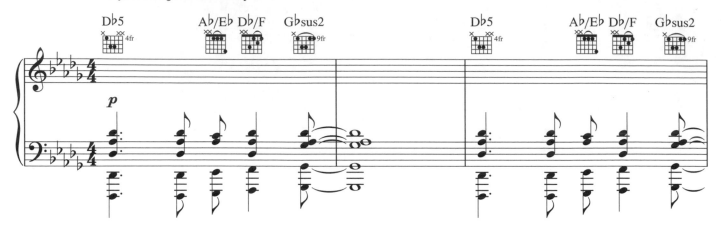

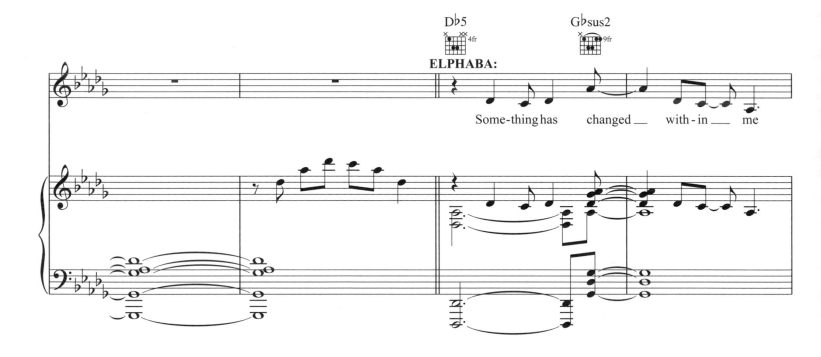

ELPHABA:
Some-thing has changed _ with-in _ me

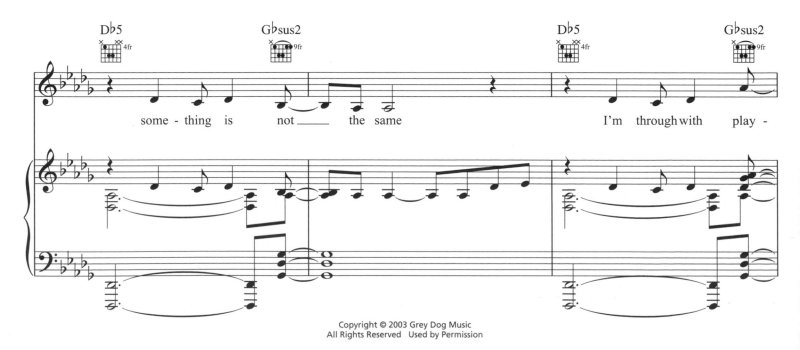

some - thing is not _ the same

I'm through with play -